DINOSAURS
OF THE MID-CRETACEOUS

DAVID & OLIVER WEST

FIREFLY BOOKS

A FIREFLY BOOK

Published by Firefly Books Ltd. 2016

First printing

Publisher Cataloging-in-Publication Data (U.S.)

Names: West, David, 1956-, author.
Title: Dinosaurs of the Middle Cretaceous : 25 dinosaurs / David West.
Description: Richmond Hill, Ontario, Canada : Firefly Books, 2016. | Series: Dinosaurs. | Includes index. | Summary: "An illustrated guide of 25 of the best-known dinosaurs of the period, providing up-to-date information with highly detailed computer generated artwork. Illustrated introductory spreads provide background information on the time periods in which the dinosaurs lived" -- Provided by publisher.
Identifiers: ISBN 978-1-77085-833-6 (paperback) | 978-1-77085-834-3 (hardcover)
Subjects: LCSH: Dinosaurs – Juvenile literature.
Classification: LCC QE861.5W478 |DDC 567.9 – dc23

Library and Archives Canada Cataloguing in Publication

CIP data for this title is available from Library and Archives Canada

Published in the United States by
Firefly Books (U.S.) Inc.
P.O. Box 1338, Ellicott Station
Buffalo, New York 14205

Published in Canada by
Firefly Books Ltd.
50 Staples Avenue, Unit 1
Richmond Hill, Ontario L4B 0A7

Printed in China

Text by David and Oliver West
Illustrations by David West

Produced by David West
Children's Books,
6 Princeton Court, 55 Felsham
Road, London SW15 1AZ

CONTENTS

THE MID-CRETACEOUS

The Mid-Cretaceous lasted from 127 to 90 million years ago when the Lower and Upper Cretaceous periods overlapped. It was far warmer than today with no ice caps at the poles. As ice caps melted sea levels began to rise, causing most of the midwest United States and parts of Europe to flood, creating new seas. South America began to draw away from Africa while India and Australia started to move away from Antarctica.

Early types of flowers appeared and had exploded into myriad forms by the end of the period. The **titanosaurs**, a group of **sauropods** that included *Argentinosaurus* and *Puertasaurus*, emerged during the second half of the period and were the largest land animals that ever lived. In the air the flying reptiles called **pterosaurs** dominated, although birds were becoming more frequent. *Hesperornis*, a flightless diving bird, preyed on fish. **Ichthyosaurs**, swimming reptiles that appeared similar to dolphins, died out by the end of this period.

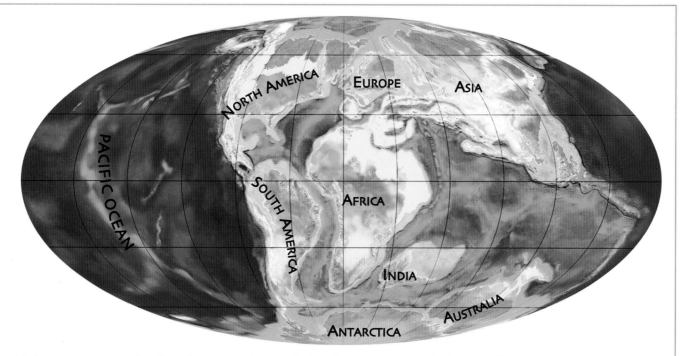

This map shows the Earth at the time of the Cretaceous period 105 million years ago.
Below, in a scene from Asia 125 million years ago, a Microraptor (1) glides through the air in
front of a group of Altirhinuses (2). A raptor (3) stalks a juvenile Psittacosaurus (4) as it runs
to the safety of its family. In the sky Zhenyuanopteruses (5) fly to feeding grounds.

ACROCANTHOSAURUS

Acrocanthosaurus means "high-spined lizard," after the tall spines along its backbone. The spines may have given it a high-arched back. It was a very large **theropod** that was capable of taking on some of the giant **sauropods** that lived at the time such as *Sauroposeidon* (see page 23). It is possible that these ferocious killers hunted in packs, using their powerful jaws to grab their prey while holding on with their clawed hands.

Acrocanthosaurus lived **115–105 million years ago**. Fossil remains have been found in the United States, North America. It grew up to 38 feet (11.5 m) long and weighed around 6.6 tons (6 tonnes).

ALTIRHINUS

Altirhinus was an **ornithopod**, closely related to *Iguanodon*. It had more teeth, a wider bill and a large, curved nose. Its name means "high nose." Scientists think it may have expanded the fleshy parts of its nose in courtship displays, like elephant seals do today.

Altirhinus lived **120–100 million years ago**. Fossil remains have been found in Mongolia, Asia. It grew up to 28 feet (8.5 m) long and weighed around 4 tons (3.6 tonnes).

ARCHAEOCERATOPS

Archaeoceratops, meaning "ancient horned face," was a direct ancestor of *Triceratops* and other "horned face" dinosaurs, although it was much smaller than other **ceratopsians**. Like all **ceratopsians** it had a frill at the back of its skull and a beak. It was a herbivore and grazed on low vegetation such as ferns. Grass had not yet evolved. It was probably bipedal, but would crouch down on all fours to feed, using its beak to snap off portions and chop them up before swallowing them.

Archaeoceratops lived between **121–99 million years ago**. Fossil remains were found in the Gansu Province of China, Asia. It grew to just over 3.3 feet (1 m) long and weighed about 30 pounds (13.6 kg).

ARGENTINOSAURUS

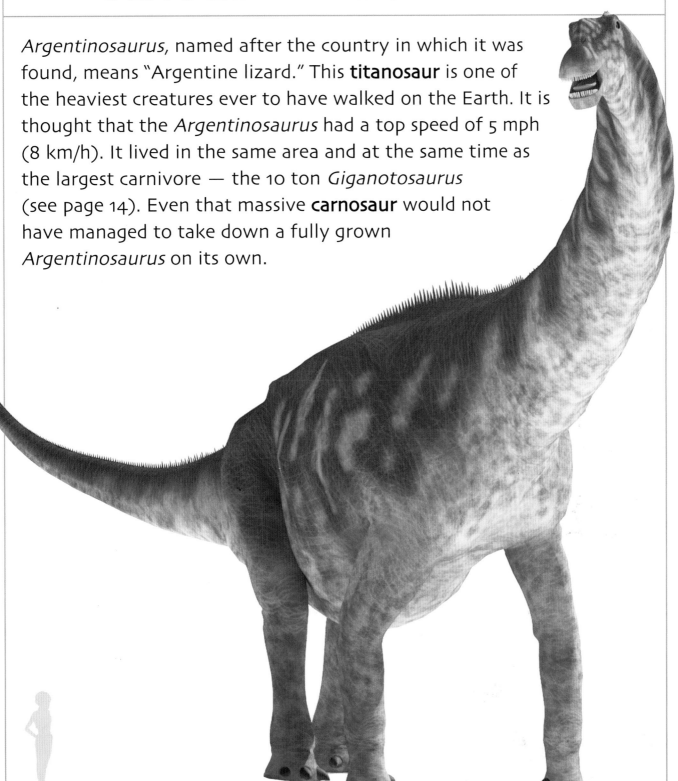

Argentinosaurus, named after the country in which it was found, means "Argentine lizard." This **titanosaur** is one of the heaviest creatures ever to have walked on the Earth. It is thought that the *Argentinosaurus* had a top speed of 5 mph (8 km/h). It lived in the same area and at the same time as the largest carnivore — the 10 ton *Giganotosaurus* (see page 14). Even that massive **carnosaur** would not have managed to take down a fully grown *Argentinosaurus* on its own.

Argentinosaurus lived between **97–94 million years ago**. Fossil remains were found in Argentina, South America. It is believed to have measured 131.2 feet (40 m) long and weighed 110 tons (100 tonnes).

DEINONYCHUS

Deinonychus was a member of the **dromaeosaur** family of dinosaurs. Its name means "terrible claw," which refers to the sickle-shaped claw on the second toe of its hind feet. Its jaws were equipped with around seventy curved, blade-like teeth. It hunted big, plant-eating dinosaurs such as *Tenontosaurus* (see page 28), using the formidable claws on its feet to stab its victims while it held on with its large hands.

Deinonychus lived **115–108 million years ago**. Fossil remains have been found in the United States, North America. It grew up to 11 feet (3.4 m) long and weighed around 165 pounds (75 kg).

DELTADROMEUS

Deltadromeus means "delta runner" and was a **theropod** dinosaur. It is known from an almost complete skeleton, although a skull has never been found. It had a slender, lightweight build with long legs and could run at high speeds. It lived in the same area and at the same time as *Spinosaurus* (see page 25), so its agility and speed were needed to help it avoid confrontations.

Deltadromeus lived **95 million years ago**. Fossil remains were found in Northern Africa. It grew up to 26.2 feet (8 m) long and weighed up to 2.2 tons (2 tonnes).

Diamantinasaurus is named after the Diamantina River in Australia, which is close to where it was found. Nicknamed "Matilda," it was fairly small for a **titanosaur**. Like all **titanosaurs** it was a quadrupedal herbivore with small bony nodules protruding from its skin. *Diamantinasaurus* was discovered alongside the **sauropod** fossils of *Wintonotitan* and *Austrosaurus*.

Diamantinasaurus lived about **94 million years ago**. Fossils were found in Queensland, Australia. It grew up to 52.5 feet (16 m) long and weighed approximately 16.5 to 22 tons (15–20 tonnes).

ERECTOPUS

Erectopus means "upright foot." It was a small **carnosaur**, related to *Allosaurus*. Like *Allosaurus*, *Erectopus* was a carnivorous **theropod** that probably hunted small, plant-eating dinosaurs. It is thought to have been one of the main predators of its ecosystem, where fossils of **ichthyosaurs** and crocodilians have also been found. This suggests that it may have lived near coastal regions of Cretaceous Europe.

Erectopus is believed to have lived around **112–99 million years ago**. Fossil remains were found in eastern France, Europe. It grew to around 9.8 feet (3 m) long and weighed about 440 pounds (200 kg).

GIGANOTOSAURUS

The "giant southern lizard" was a huge, meat-eating **theropod** that stood more than 16.4 feet (5 m) tall. Its jaw was lined with long, blade-like, serrated teeth that were ideal for slicing through meat. These giant predators may have hunted the large **sauropod**, *Argentinosaurus* (see page 9).

Giganotosaurus lived **112–90 million years ago**. Fossil remains have been found in Argentina, South America. It grew up to 41 feet (12.5 m) long and weighed around 6.6 to 8.8 tons (6–8 tonnes).

LURDUSAURUS

Lurdusaurus means "heavy lizard" due to its strangely robust build and skeleton. Like *Iguanodon*, *Lurdusaurus* had a large thumb spike and a broad break. The thumb spike may have been used for defense against predators. It had relatively short legs compared with other **ornithopods**, and it is thought it had large fleshy pads on its feet to help support its immense weight. It has been suggested that *Lurdusaurus* had an aquatic lifestyle similar to today's hippopotamuses.

Lurdusaurus lived between **121–112 million years ago**. Fossils were found in Niger, Africa. It grew up to 29.5 feet (9 m) long and weighed up to 6.1 tons (5.5 tonnes).

Mapusaurus, meaning "earth lizard," was a huge **carnosaur theropod**, and a close relative of *Giganotosaurus* (see page 14). Fossils of seven individuals were found together in a bone bed. They varied in age and size, suggesting that *Mapusaurus*, and possibly other **carnosaurs**, hunted in packs. *Mapusaurus* might have hunted the large **titanosaur** *Argentinosaurus* (see page 9). Its curved, serrated teeth were ideal for slicing through flesh.

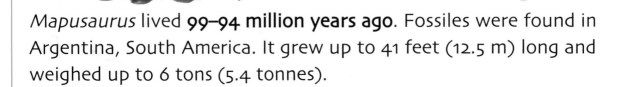

Mapusaurus lived **99–94 million years ago**. Fossiles were found in Argentina, South America. It grew up to 41 feet (12.5 m) long and weighed up to 6 tons (5.4 tonnes).

MICRORAPTOR

Microraptor, meaning "small hunter," was one of the smallest dinosaurs of the **dromaeosaur** family. Well-preserved fossils show that it was covered in feathers, with wing-like feathers on its arms and legs. Scientists believe that it spent most of its life in trees, using its clawed hands and feet to climb up the tree trunk. From this lofty position it would launch itself into the air to glide to the next tree, using its tail to steer. It would have fed on small mammals, lizards and insects.

Microraptor lived **125–120 million years ago**. Fossil remains have been found in China, Asia. It was very small and light, growing up to only 3 feet (0.9 m) long and weighing, less than 2 pounds (1 kg).

OURANOSAURUS

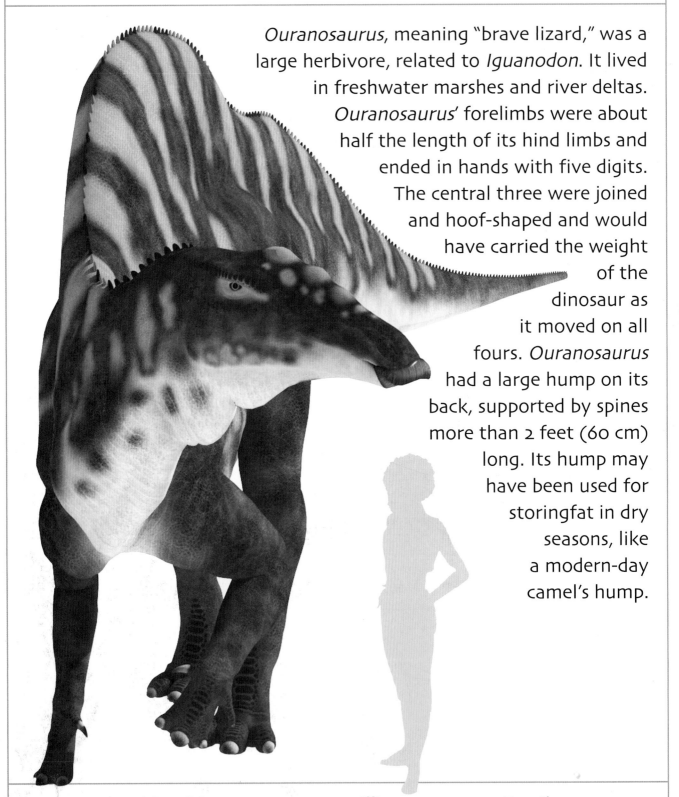

Ouranosaurus, meaning "brave lizard," was a large herbivore, related to *Iguanodon*. It lived in freshwater marshes and river deltas. *Ouranosaurus'* forelimbs were about half the length of its hind limbs and ended in hands with five digits. The central three were joined and hoof-shaped and would have carried the weight of the dinosaur as it moved on all fours. *Ouranosaurus* had a large hump on its back, supported by spines more than 2 feet (60 cm) long. Its hump may have been used for storingfat in dry seasons, like a modern-day camel's hump.

Ouranosaurus lived between **125–112 million years ago**. Fossils were found in Niger, Africa. It grew up to 27 feet (8.3 m) long and weighed between 2.2 and 4.4 tons (2–4 tonnes).

PSITTACOSAURUS

The "parrot lizard" was a small, early type of **ceratopsian** dinosaur that lived in large herds. It used its beak to crop a meal of vegetation that was then chewed, swallowed and ground between stones, called gastroliths, in its gizzard. Although it is shown on all four legs here, paleontologists believe that some of the 10 or so species of *Psittacosaurus* currently known walked or ran on two legs.

Psittacosaurus lived **123–100 million years ago**. Fossil remains have been found in Thailand, China, and Mongolia, Asia. It grew between 3.3 and 6.6 feet (1–2 m) in length and weighed around 44 pounds (20 kg).

PUERTASAURUS

Puertasaurus, named after the paleontologist Pablo Puerta who found its fossils, was a **titanosaur**. Along with *Argentinosaurus* (see page 9), it was possibly the longest but almost certainly the widest and heaviest of all dinosaurs. Its neck was also remarkable. Judging from the single neck vertebra found so far, it might have able to bend backward to reach higher vegetation behind its head, although it probably had less flexibility from side to side.

Puertasaurus lived **97 million years ago**. Fossils were found in Patagonia in South America. It grew up to 131 feet (40 m) long and weighed in the region of 88 to 110 tons (80–100 tonnes).

SANTANARAPTOR

Santanaraptor is named after the area where it was found in Brazil, South America. It means "Santana thief." It was a carnivorous **theropod** of the **coelurosaur** family. The *Santanaraptor* had long front arms with three elongated fingers that were perfect for grasping and holding onto prey, and long claws capable of delivering deep wounds. Its rear limbs were slender and long, propelling it to great speeds. It is believed to be similar to *Dilong* and *Guanlong*. The fossil specimen found is very special, since it contained fossilized soft tissue. This gives an insight into the animal's muscle fibers and possibly into its blood vessels, too.

Santanaraptor lived about **115–110 million years ago**. Its fossil remains were found in northeastern Brazil, South America. It grew up to around 4.1 feet (1.25 m) long and weighed 40 pounds (18.1 kg).

SAUROPELTA

Sauropelta means "lizard shield" after its covering of leathery, armored skin. It was a **nodosaur** — a member of the **ankylosaurs**. It had no club on the end of its tail but was well armored, with tough, bony nodules along its back and four large spikes running down each side of its neck. Two of these spikes were very long and could have deterred predators such as *Acrocanthosaurus* (see page 6).

Sauropelta lived **115–108 million years ago**. Fossil remains were found in the United States, North America. It is believed to have grown up to 16.4 feet (4.9 m) long and weighed approximately 300 pounds (136 kg).

SAUROPOSEIDON

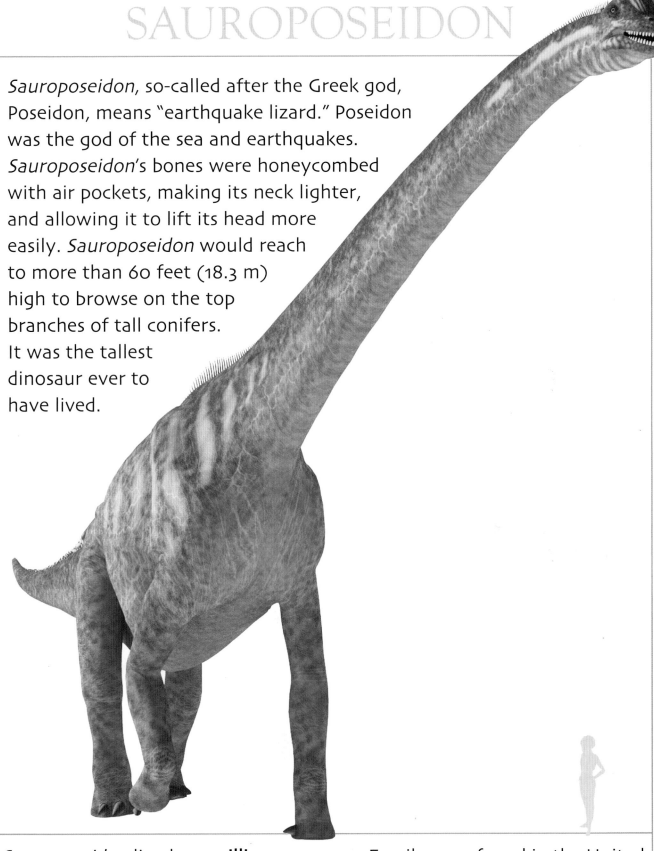

Sauroposeidon, so-called after the Greek god, Poseidon, means "earthquake lizard." Poseidon was the god of the sea and earthquakes. *Sauroposeidon*'s bones were honeycombed with air pockets, making its neck lighter, and allowing it to lift its head more easily. *Sauroposeidon* would reach to more than 60 feet (18.3 m) high to browse on the top branches of tall conifers. It was the tallest dinosaur ever to have lived.

Sauroposeidon lived **110 million years ago**. Fossils were found in the United States, North America. It is estimated to have grown up to 112 feet (34 m) long and weighed approximately 55 to 66 tons (50–60 tonnes).

SHUANGMIAOSAURUS

Shuangmiaosaurus is named after the village where it was found — Shuangmiao in Liaoning Province in China, Asia. It was a large **iguanodont** with forelimbs that were shorter than its hindlimbs. It was a quadrupedal herbivore, but like most **iguanodonts** it could rear onto its hind legs. It used its beak to browse on low vegetation.

Shuangmiaosaurus lived **100 million years ago**. Fossils were found in Liaoning Province in China, Asia. It would have grown up to 24.6 feet (7.5 m) long and weighed approximately 2.8 tons (2.5 tonnes).

Spinosaurus, meaning "spine lizard," was the largest, meat-eating **theropod** dinosaur, bigger even than *Tyrannosaurus*. It had tall spines growing from its back that formed a large sail. Scientists think the sail was used to control the dinosaur's temperature, like a radiator in a car. It probably hunted aquatic animals in the rivers and swamps where it lived.

Spinosaurus lived **112–   million years ago**. Fossil remains have been found in Egypt and Morocco in Africa. It grew up to 59 feet (18 m) long and weighed around 22 tons (20 tonnes).

SUCHOMIMUS

The "crocodile mimic" was a large, meat-eating **spinosaur** dinosaur with a crocodile-like skull. *Suchomimus'* jaws were lined with about 122 slightly backward-facing, conical teeth. They were ideal for catching fish and other aquatic prey in the swampy habitat where *Suchomimus* lived. Its strong forelimbs, with a huge, sickle-curved claw on each thumb, helped to keep hold of its slippery prey.

Suchomimus lived **121–113 million years ago**. Fossil remains have been found in Niger, Africa. It grew up to 36 feet (11 m) long and weighed around 5 tons (4.5 tonnes).

Talarurus, meaning "wicker tail" or "basket tail," was named after the powerful tendons in its tail that resembled wicker work. Its tail ended in a club, which it used to smash into the legs of predators that got too close. It was a heavily armored dinosaur of the same group as **ankylosaurs**. It was about the size of a hippopotamus, had four short legs and grazed on low-lying plants. Its armored back and neck were covered in short spikes.

Talarurus lived approximately **90 million years ago**. Fossil remains have been found in Mongolia, Asia. It could grow up to 19.7 feet (6 m) long and weighed up to 2.2 tons (2 tonnes).

TENONTOSAURUS

Tenontosaurus was a primitive **iguanodont**. Its name means "sinew lizard," after the powerful tendons that were needed to keep its impressive tail off the ground at all times. The tail was long and broad, and was more than half the length of its body. Its long forelimbs and strong fingerbones suggest *Tenontosaurus* was probably a quadruped, but would have been able to rear onto its hind legs, using its tail as a counter-weight. This way it could have fed on higher vegetation.

Tenontosaurus lived between **115–108 million years ago**. Fossil remains have been found all over the Western United States, North America. It could grow up to 26 feet (8 m) long and weighed up to 2.2 tons (2 tonnes).

UTAHRAPTOR

The "thief from Utah" is the largest known member of the **dromaeosaurs**, which were a family of bird-like **theropod** dinosaurs. Like other **dromaeosaurs**, *Utahraptors* had large curved claws on their second toes that measured up to 9.4 inches (24 cm) long. They kept their claws raised so they would not become blunted on the ground as they ran. The claws were used to stab their prey as they held onto them with their clawed hands. Recent discoveries have suggested that these dinosaurs were warm-blooded and were coated in feathers to keep them warm.

Utahraptor lived around **126 million years ago**. Fossil remains have been found in the United States, North America. It grew to an estimated 23 feet (7 m) long and weighed around 1,100 pounds (500 kg).

ZUNICERATOPS

Named after the Zuni Native Indians of New Mexico, United States, where it was found, *Zuniceratops* means "Zuni-horned face." It is the earliest known **ceratopsian** dinosaur, and the similarities to *Triceratops* are clear. *Zuniceratops* had two distinctive brow horns, which grew longer with age, and a large, bone frill that had two holes in it covered with skin. This frill was probably used as a display to other *Zuniceratopses*.

Zuniceratops lived between **94–89 million years ago**. Fossil remains have been found in the United States, North America. It would grow to around 11.5 feet (3.5 m) long and weighed up to 330 pounds (150 kg).

GLOSSARY

ankylosaur
A family of bulky quadrupedal, armored dinosaurs that had a clublike tail. The family included *Ankylosaurus* and *Euoplocephalus*.

carnosaur
A member of a group of large predatory dinosaurs, encompassing all the allosaurs.

ceratopsian
A member of a group of herbivorous, beaked dinosaurs with frilled collars. Members include *Triceratops*.

coelurosaur
A member of a group of theropod dinosaurs more closely related to birds than to carnosaurs.

dromaeosaur
A family of bird-like theropod dinosaurs with a large, curved claw on the second toe, which included the famous *Velociraptor*.

ichthyosaur
A dolphin-like reptile that lived in the oceans.

iguanodont
A group of herbivorous dinosaurs, including duck-billed dinosaurs.

nodosaur
A member of the ankylosaurs which does not have a clubbed tail.

ornithopod
A group of herbivorous, running grazers.

oviraptosaur
A member of a group of carnivorous egg thieves, characterized by their short, beaked skulls.

pterosaur
Flying reptiles that include *Pterodactylus*.

sauropod
A group of large, four-legged, herbivorous dinosaurs with long necks and long tails. This group included the well-known *Brachiosaurus* and *Diplodocus*.

spinosaur
A group of large carnivorous theropods with crocodile-like skulls, often with a large sail on their backs—includes *Spinosaurus*.

theropod
The large group of lizard-hipped dinosaurs that walked on two legs and included most of the giant carnivores such as *Tyrannosaurus*.

titanosaur
A family of sauropod dinosaurs that included some of the heaviest animals ever to walk the Earth such as *Argentinosaurus*.

INDEX